Wild Ride

Judy East Wells

Wild Ride

Judy East Wells

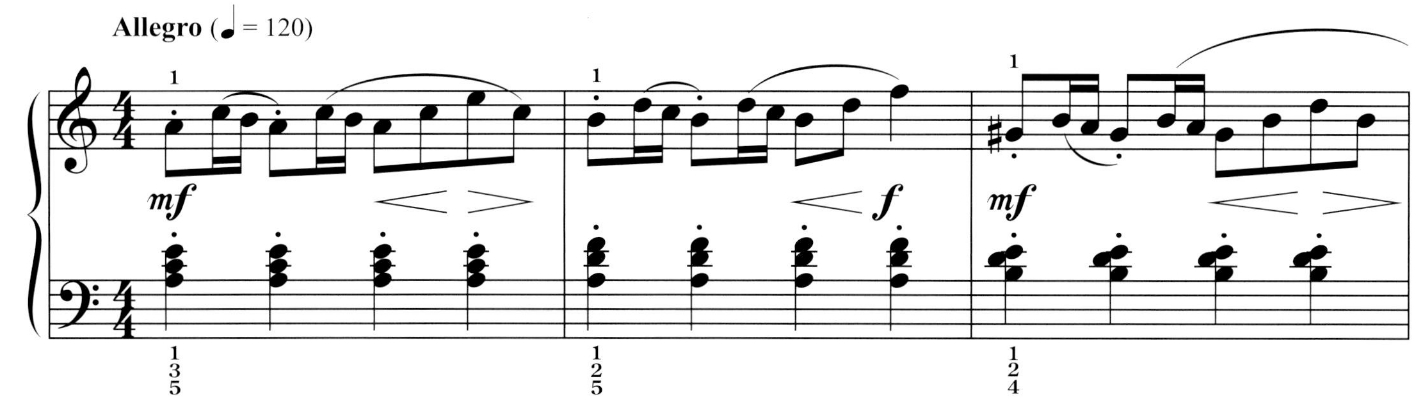

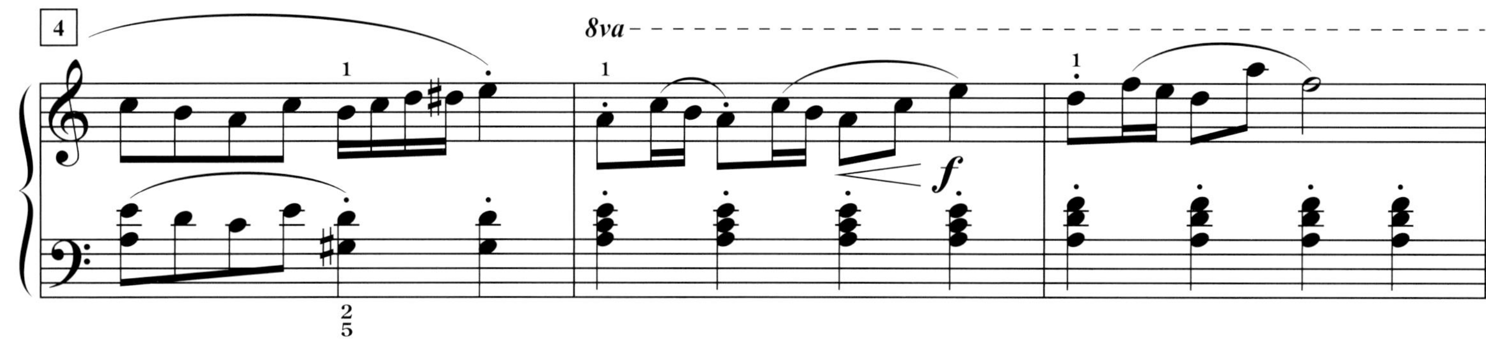

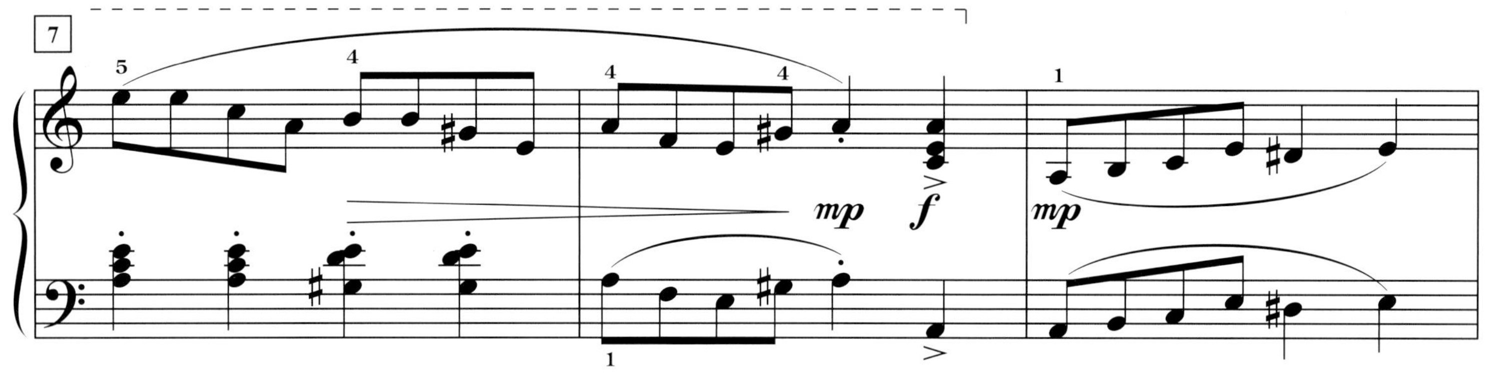

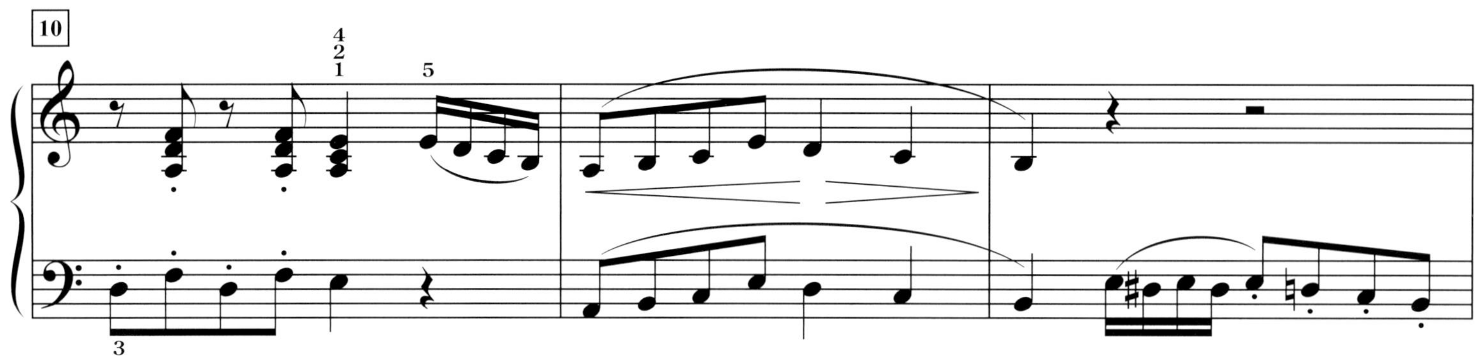

Copyright © MMIX by Alfred Music Publishing Co., Inc.
All rights reserved. Printed in USA.

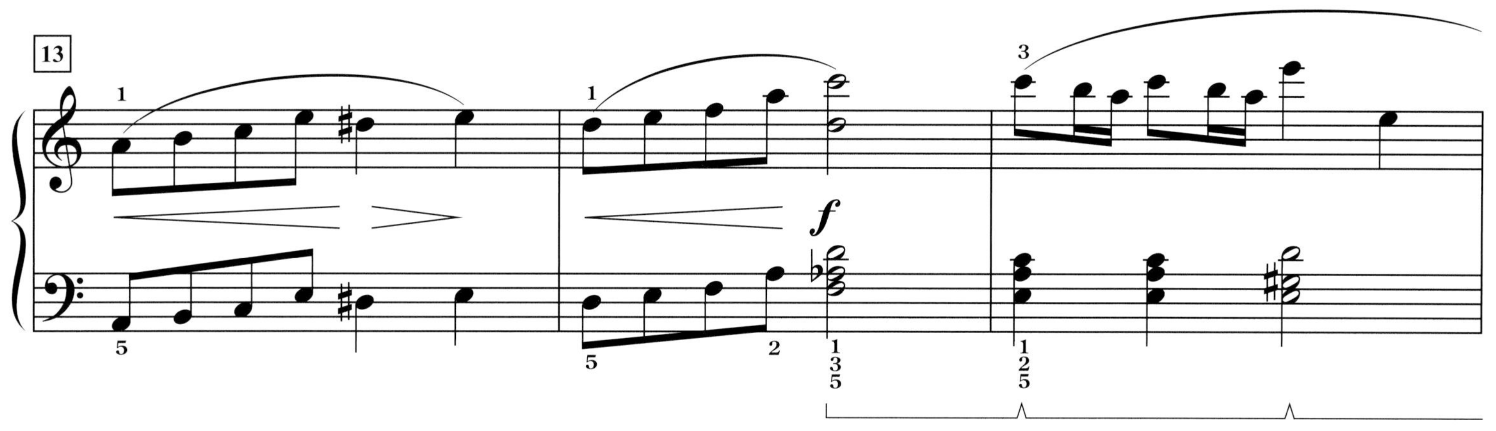

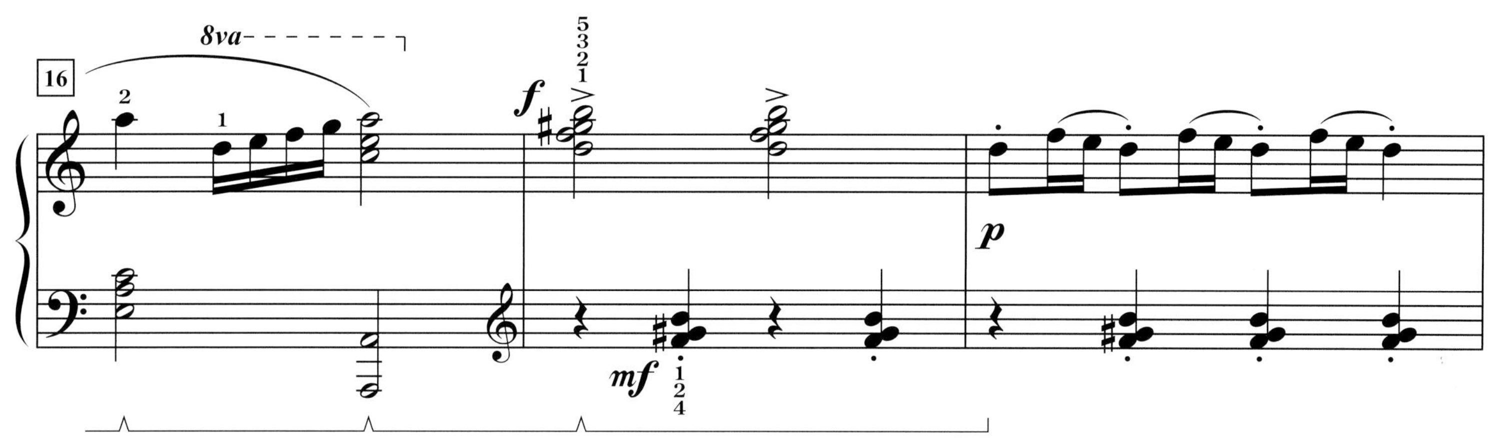

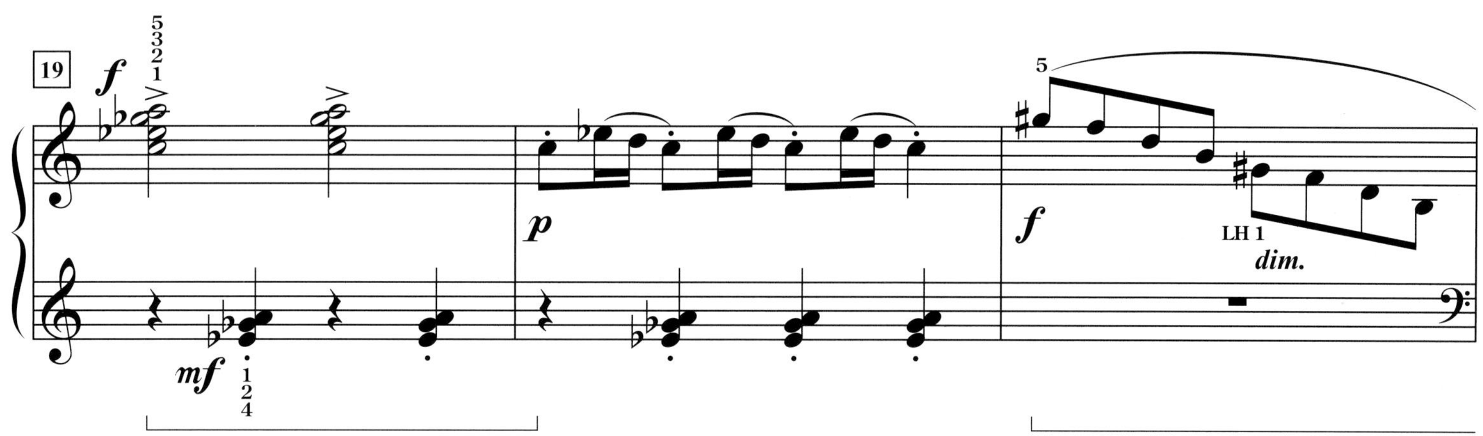

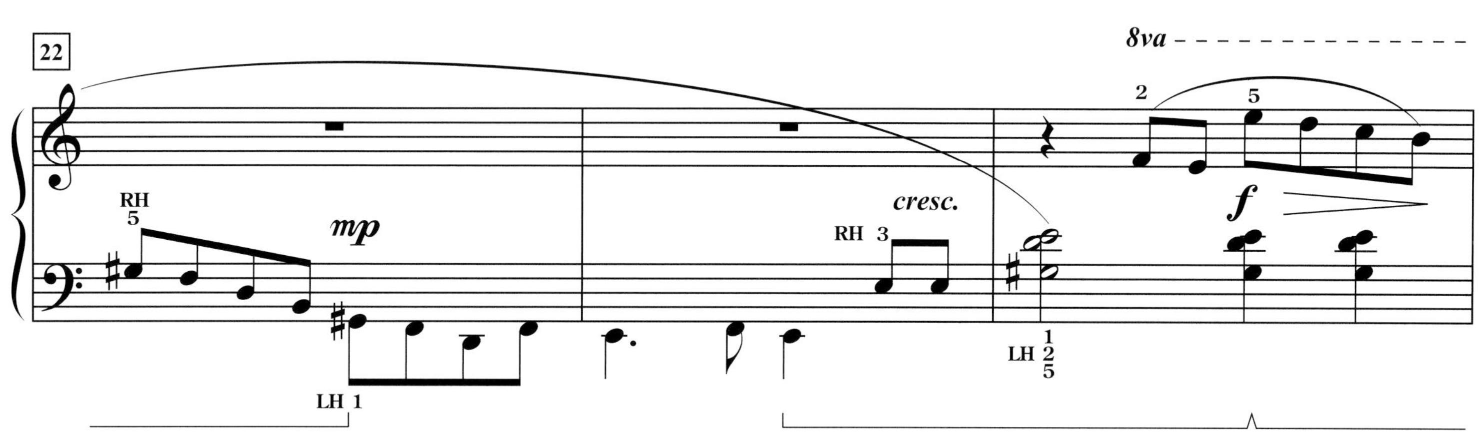

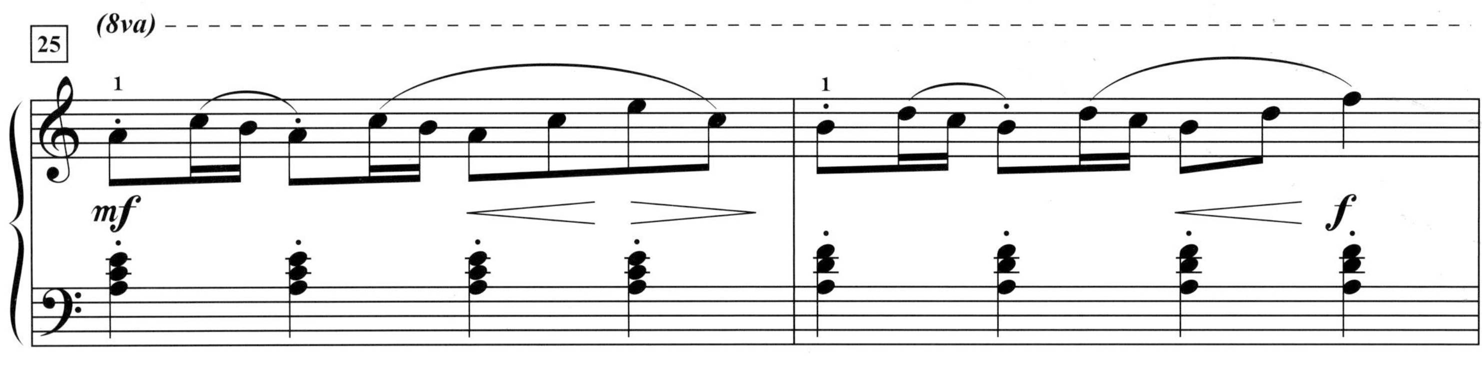

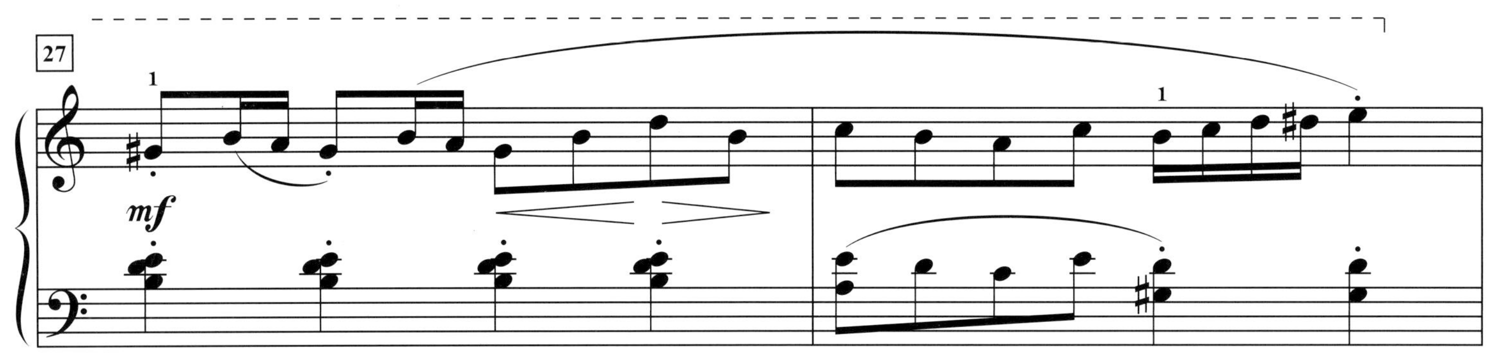

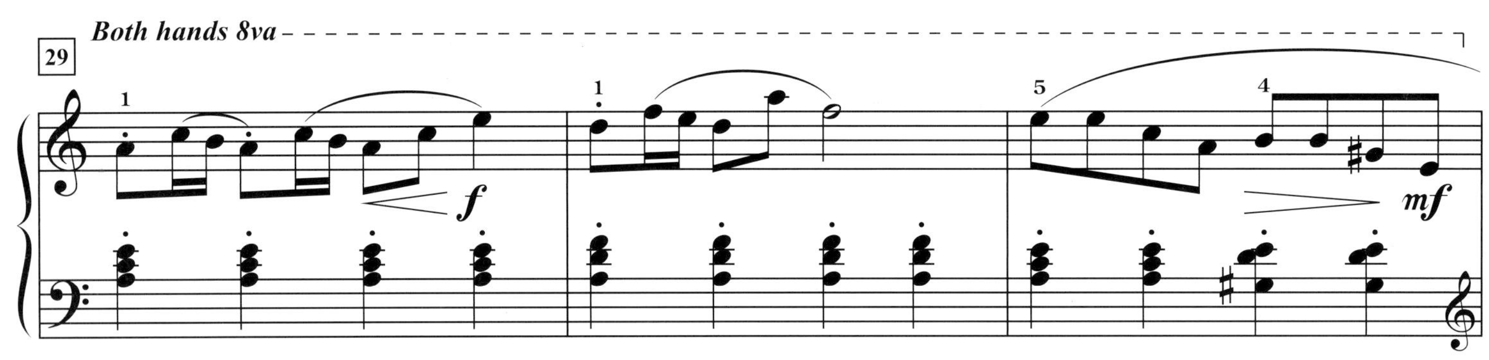

Wild Ride • Wells

Alfred

34306   US $2.95

ISBN-10: 0-7390-6628-5
ISBN-13: 978-0-7390-6628-7

50295

0 38081 38079 7

9 780739 066287